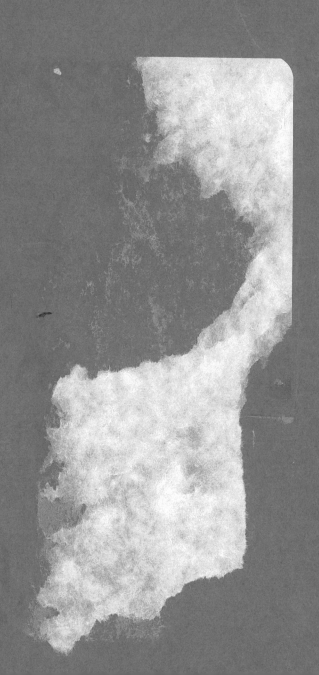

THIS LITTLE PIG-A-WIG

THIS LITTLE PIG-A-WIG

AND OTHER RHYMES ABOUT PIGS

Chosen by
Lenore Blegvad

Illustrated by
Erik Blegvad

A Margaret K. McElderry Book

ATHENEUM 1978 NEW YORK

Library of Congress catalog card number 78-7015
ISBN 0-689-50110-2
Published simultaneously in Canada by McClelland & Stewart, Ltd.
Printed in Great Britain
Bound by A. Horowitz & Son/Bookbinders
Clifton, New Jersey
First Edition

The verses in this book are taken from the following sources: *The Barnes Book of Nursery Verse* edited by Barbara Ireson— "As I looked out" "A little pig"; *The London Treasury of Nursery Rhymes* collected by J. Murray MacBain—"The little farmer" "Little Dame Crump"; *Mother Goose's Melodies,* Facsimile Edition of 1833—"The sow came in with the saddle"; *The Nursery Rhymes of England* collected by James Orchard Halliwell—"Dickery, dickery, dare" "Little Jack Dandy-prat" "Come dance a jig" "To market, to market"; *The Oxford Dictionary of Nursery Rhymes* edited by Iona and Peter Opie— "Let's go to the wood" "This pig got in the barn"; *The Oxford Nursery Rhyme Book* assembled by Iona and Peter Opie—"This little pig-a-wig" "Little Jack Sprat" "Lazy Elsie Marley" "Little Betty Pringle" "Whose little pigs" "Pastry pigs for sale" "Tom, Tom" "Sukey, you shall be my wife" "Grandfa' Grig"; *Trotting to Market—Poems for Infants* chosen by Noel Holmes—"My Uncle Jehosaphat."

THIS LITTLE PIG-A-WIG

This little pig had a rub-a-dub,
This little pig had a scrub-a-scrub,
This little pig-a-wig ran upstairs,
This little pig-a-wig called out, Bears!
Down came the jar with a loud
   Slam! Slam!
And this little pig had all the jam.

LITTLE JACK SPRAT

Little Jack Sprat
Once had a pig;
It was not very little,
Nor yet very big,
It was not very lean,
It was not very fat—
It's a good pig to grunt,
Said little Jack Sprat.

LET'S GO TO THE WOOD

Let's go to the wood, says this pig,
What to do there? says that pig,
To look for my mother, says this pig,
What to do with her? says that pig,
Kiss her to death, says this pig.

DICKERY, DICKERY, DARE

Dickery, dickery, dare,
The pig flew up in the air;
The man in brown soon brought him down,
Dickery, dickery, dare.

LAZY ELSIE MARLEY

Elsie Marley is grown so fine
She won't get up to serve the swine,
But lies in bed till eight or nine,
Lazy Elsie Marley.

LITTLE BETTY PRINGLE

Little Betty Pringle she had a pig,
It was not very little and not very big;
When it was alive it lived in clover,
But now it's dead and that's all over.
Johnny Pringle he sat down and cried,
Betty Pringle she lay down and died;
So there was an end of one, two, three,
Johnny Pringle, Betty Pringle she,
    And Piggy Wiggy.

THIS LITTLE PIGGY WENT TO MARKET

This little piggy went to market,
This little piggy stayed home,

This little piggy had roast beef,
This little piggy had none,

And this little piggy cried, wee, wee, wee,
All the way home.

MY UNCLE JEHOSAPHAT

My uncle Jehosaphat had a pig,
A pig of high degree;
And it always wore a brown scratch wig,
Most beautiful for to see.

My uncle Jehosaphat loved that pig,
And the piggy-wig he loved him;
And they both jumped into the lake one day,
To see which best could swim.

My uncle Jehosaphat he swam up
And the piggy-wig he swam down;
And so they both did win the prize,
Which the same was a velvet gown.

WHOSE LITTLE PIGS

Whose little pigs are these, these, these?
Whose little pigs are these?
They are Roger the Cook's, I know by their looks:
I found them among my peas.
Go pound them, go pound them.
I dare not on my life,
For though I love not Roger the Cook,
I dearly love his wife.

THE SOW CAME IN WITH THE SADDLE

The sow came in with the saddle,
The little pig rocked the cradle,
The dish jumped up on the table
To see the pot swallow the ladle.
The spit that stood behind the door
Threw the pudding-stick on the floor.
Odsplut! said the gridiron,
Can't you agree?
I'm the head constable,
Bring them to me.

THE LITTLE FARMER

Once there lived a little man
Where a little river ran,
And he had a little farm and a little dairy, O.
And he had a little plough,
And a little dappled cow,
Which he often called his pretty little fairy, O.

And his dog he called Fidèle,
For he loved his master well,
And he had a little pony for his pleasure, O!
In a sty, not very big,
He'd a frisky little pig
Which he often called his little piggy treasure, O!

AS I LOOKED OUT

As I looked out on Saturday last,
A fat little pig went hurrying past.
Over his shoulders he wore a shawl,
Although it didn't seem cold at all.
I waved at him, but he didn't see,
For he never so much as looked at me.

Once again, when the moon was high,
I saw the little pig hurrying by;
Back he came at a terrible pace,
The moonlight shone on his little pink face,
And he smiled with a smile that was quite content.
But never I knew where that little pig went.

PASTRY PIGS FOR SALE

A long-tailed pig,
Or a short-tailed pig,
Or a pig without any tail;
A sow pig,
Or a boar pig,
Or a pig with a curly tail.
Take hold of the tail
And eat off his head,
And then you'll be sure
The pig-hog is dead.

TOM, TOM

Tom, Tom, the piper's son,
Stole a pig and away he run;
The pig was eat,
And Tom was beat,
And Tom went howling down the street.

A LITTLE PIG

A little pig found a fifty-dollar note,
And purchased a hat and a very fine coat,
With trousers, and stockings, and shoes;
Cravat, and shirt collar and gold-headed cane;
Then, proud as could be, did he march up the lane;
Says he, "I shall hear all the news."

SUKEY, YOU SHALL BE MY WIFE

Sukey, you shall be my wife
And I will tell you why:
I have got a little pig,
And you have got a sty;
I have got a dun cow,
And you can make good cheese;
Sukey, will you marry me?
Say Yes, if you please.

LITTLE JACK DANDY-PRAT

Little Jack Dandy-prat was my first suitor;
He had a dish and a spoon, and he'd some pewter;
He'd linen and woollen, and woollen and linen,
A little pig in a string cost him five shilling.

COME DANCE A JIG

Come dance a jig,
To my granny's pig,
With a raudy, rowdy, dowdy;
Come dance a jig
To my granny's pig,
And pussy-cat shall crowdy.

LITTLE DAME CRUMP

Little Dame Crump, with her little hair broom,
One morning was sweeping her little bedroom,
When, casting her little grey eyes on the ground,
In a sly little corner a penny she found.

"Ods bobs!" cried the Dame, while she stared with surprise,
"How lucky I am! bless my heart, what a prize!
To market I'll go, and a pig I will buy,
And little John Gubbins shall make him a stye."

So she washed her face clean, and put on her gown,
And locked up the house, and set off for the town;
When to market she went, and a purchase she made
Of a little white pig, and a penny she paid.

When she'd purchased the pig, she was puzzled to know
How they both should get home, if the pig would not go;
So fearing lest piggie should play her a trick,
She drove him along with a little crab stick.

Piggy ran till they came to the foot of a hill,
Where a little bridge stood o'er the stream of a mill;
Piggie grunted and squealed, but no farther would go:
Oh fie! Piggie, fie! to serve little Dame so.

She went to the mill, and she borrowed a sack
To put the pig in, and took him on her back;
Piggie squeaked to get out, but the little Dame said,
"If you won't go by fair means, why you must be made."

At last to the end of her journey she came,
And was mightily glad when she got the pig hame;
She carried him straight to his nice little stye,
And gave him some hay and clean straw nice and dry.

With a handful of peas then Piggie she fed,
And put on her nightcap and got into bed;
Having first said her prayers, she extinguished the light,
And being quite tired, we'll wish her goodnight.

TO MARKET, TO MARKET

To market, to market, to buy a fat pig,
Home again, home again, dancing a jig;
Ride to the market to buy a fat hog,
Home again, home again, jiggety-jog.

THIS PIG GOT IN THE BARN

This pig got in the barn,
This ate all the corn,
This said he wasn't well,
This said he would go and tell,
And this said—weke, weke, weke,
I can't get over the barn door sill.

GRANDFA' GRIG

Grandfa' Grig
Had a pig,
In a field of clover;
Piggy died,
Grandfa' cried,
And all the fun was over.